A WILD GOOSE CHASE

© 2016 by Karen Stanley. All rights reserved.
Story by Karen Stanley
Illustrated by Mia Watson & Scott Burchell

Thanks to Mia Watson for her original drawings that brought The Wild Goose Chase to life

ISBN: 978-0-9934439-9-2

The pig was porky,
The dog was dapper,
The sheep was sharp,
The duck, a flapper.

The horse was hefty,
The cat was cute,
The goat was gracious,
The cockerel... a beaut!

But the goose was grumpy,
His temper was foul,
He hissed, and he squawked,
He grunted and growled.

No matter what day,
What time or place,
The animals ran,
While the goose gave chase.

The pig tried to tempt him,
With scraps from his trough,
But the goose flapped his wings,
And chased him right off.

The dog tried to please him,
With jokes and a dance,
But the goose made him scared,
With his threatening stance.

The cock tried to wow him,
With his outstanding beauty,
But the goose made a noise,
All angry and hooty.

"Enough" said the cat,
"I'm sick of that grump,
His temper and tanturms,
Put us down in the dump!"

"I agree," said the duck,
His feathers a-fluster,
"That goose is too much,
With his brawn and his bluster."

"We need a plan,"
Said the sheep who was sharp,
"This time that old goose,
Has gone much too far."

"He needs to chill out,"
Said the horse who was hefty,
"We need to teach him;
And do it deftly."

"Right," said the goat,
Who was ever so gracious,
"His love of violence
Is becoming voracious."

So the animals huddled,
They schemed and conspired,
They planned and they plotted,
'Till they really were tired.

The very next day,
While the sun was still sleeping,
The animal crew,
From the barn they were peeping.

They crept through the yard,
All brave and stealthy,
"I fear," said the duck,
"This may not be healthy!"

"Ssssh!" said his chums,
"Don't lose your nerve,
That goose needs a lesson,
One he deserves!"

The goose unaware,
Was asleep by the rushes,
When the pig (who was first)
Leapt out from the bushes.

He oinked and he oinked,
'Till his throat was quite sore,
The goose woke with a start,
And began to ROAR!

The porky old pig,
Ran off at a pace,
With the goose close behind
As he gave chase.

The plump little pig,
Ran 'till he dropped,
and the dog took over,
From where he had stopped.

The dog did a dance,
And pulled a rude face,
And the goose in a frenzy,
Continued the chase.

The dog was fast,
He ran 'till he dropped,
And the sheep took over,
From where he had stopped.

The sheep was not scared,
With his fleece so woolly,
He blew a raspberry
At the angry goose bully.

The sheep was not fast,
But he ran 'till he dropped,
And the duck took over,
From where he had stopped.

The duck flapped around,
As he usually did,
And the goose was so mad,
He near flipped his lid!

The duck didn't run,
He flew 'till he dropped,
And the horse took over,
From where he had stopped.

Now by this time,
The goose was flagging,
From squawking and chasing,
He really was lagging.

The horse galloped on,
And he never dropped,
And no-one took over,
'Cos he never stopped.

He cantered through fields,
At a furious pace,
As the tired old goose,
Gave less of a chase.

They came to a stream,
The horse cleared in one jump,
But the goose tripped and stumbled,
And collapsed with a bump.

"Ha, Ha!" said the animals,
"Now will you stop?"
But the goose only nodded,
His breath was used up!

"I've learned my lesson,"
The goose puffed and wheezed,
"If I carry on chasing,
I'll end up deceased."

"Good," said the cat,
"We could always be friends,"
"Yes," said the cockerel,
"If you make amends."

"There's no point to your anger,
Your hiss and cross face,
And no good ever comes,
Of a wild goose chase!"

www.ingramcontent.com/pod-product-compliance
Lightning Source LLC
Chambersburg PA
CBHW041659040426

42452CB00022B/2977